★ NEW ★

KING PHILIP'S WAR

KING PHILIP'S WAR

a poem

By Sheppard Ranbom

Sections of *King Philip's War* originally appeared in *The Independent Scholar*. The map on page 7 is from *King Philip's War: Civil War in New England, 1675–1676* by James D. Drake, copyright © 1999 by the University of Massachusetts Press and is reprinted with permission.

Special thanks to Mel Grant, Larry Moffi, Angus Paul, Jeffrey Ranbom, M. Sandra Reeves, and E. Michael Thron.

Library of Congress Catalogue-in-Publication Data
Ranbom, Sheppard
King philip's war
ISBN: 978-0-615-20890-9

First edition

Manufactured in the United States of America

Book design by A. Good Man Designs

SETTLEMENT HOUSE
www.settlementhouse.us
2200 Wilson Blvd., Suite 102 #184
Arlington, VA 22201-3324

In memory of Alfred Ranbom
(1925-2005)

King Philip, aka Metacom or Metacomet (1638-1676), a Wampanoag chief, led the confederation of Algonquian tribes in New England. Philip fought against the English colonists and members of other tribes in what has been described as the bloodiest war in American history. This piece is an extended lyric—a work of memory and imagination—not history. It must be so, for Philip is as much a phantom to historians as he was to the soldiers who hunted him.

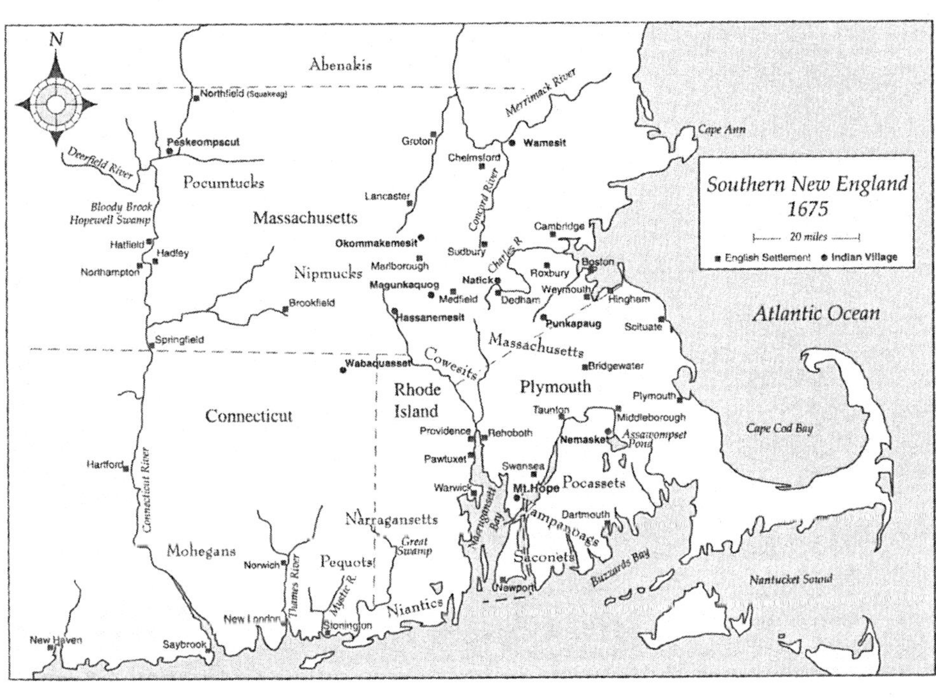

N
Abenakis
Northfield (Squakeag)
Merrimack River
Cape Ann
Peskeompscut
Groton
Wamesit
Deerfield River
Chelmsford
Southern New England
1675
20 miles
English Settlement
Indian Village
Pocumtucks
Concord River
Lancaster
Bloody Brook
Hopewell Swamp
Massachusetts
Cambridge
Okommakemesit
Sudbury
Charles R.
Hatfield
Hadley
Northampton
Nipmucks
Marlborough
Roxbury
Boston
Magunkaquog
Natick
Weymouth
Medfield
Dedham
Hingham
Brookfield
Hassanemesit
Punkapaug
Scituate
Atlantic Ocean
Springfield
Massachusetts
Wabaquasset
Cowesits
Bridgewater
Rhode
Island
Plymouth
Plymouth
Connecticut
Taunton
Middleborough
Providence
Rehoboth
Nemasket
Assawompset
Pond
Cape Cod Bay
Hartford
Pawtuxet
Swansea
Connecticut River
Warwick
Mt.Hope
Pocassets
Narragansetts
Dartmouth
Narragansett Bay
Wampanoags
Great
Swamp
Mohegans
Norwich
Pequots
Thames River
Saconets
Mystic R.
Newport
Buzzards Bay
Nantucket Sound
Niantics
New London
Stonington
New Haven
Saybrook

Contents

King Philip's War

Prologue

The spirits travel on a string of sound
hovering in the cold vapor of the morning air
heard here in this ominous knell–
the sound of eternity in an empty shell.

I WAS A KING, not of Greece or Rome
or of the tall spires of Christendom
whose many factions bloodied Europe's
messy room, but of the hills and brooks

around my home: followers of Massasoit,
sachem of the Wampanoag. I, Metacom,
his second son, broke a century's calm
and scourged towns from Albany to Montaup.

Perhaps you have seen me along the road,
a sunning coil of beaded bone and skin,
a cold-fanged viper, hungry
for the blood of your firstborn.

The Mathers painted me rogue,
then paid for Mosely's pirates to fill
their slaver's hulls with red meat
and eggs from my nest. What was safe?

The English saw my ghost in ears
of corn, my breath in every larch.
My people took to swamp—relearning arts
of siege and war—to live on tubers

and shoot the silent bow, to move in secret
until a squaw *sachem*, drunk for reward,
gave up the fort. At Pokanoket they
butchered me, a Sakonnet posting my nob

on Church's pike in Druid victory,
my skull carried to Plymouth where it stood
twenty years as a totem of English brotherhood.
Tongue-less, with no cord, I speak

from the dung and arrow bones,
the slag hills and tobacco barns,
and the blustering, minty birch—
speak not as revenge's renegade,

but as victim of a tragedy played
to genocide: I was America's first terrorist,
the cause of every loss and wrong,
and martyr for the thousands gone.

See my skull. The grim specter
of my battered crown is my scepter.
Nummeneshánnantam! I shout
my whooping battle cry

scoring empire and theocracy
and lands taken by divine decree,
and all Cotton-mouthed statesmen
whose words are not God's, but Satan's,

saying: "This land is my garden, heaven's gift
by His will taken." Searching for what is sovereign
we trespass others, fall from grace
on the tightrope between *Manitou* and man.

So let us walk on moccasin feet
following the past's collective path,
over stones and trails still there to read,
as passionate as the centuries.

THEIR WAYS WERE strange. Not their clothes, utensils,
the riches in their pockets, or their means of travel—
the high-masted ships a squall would easily buffet
into our harbors. They were shiftless, shifty

as the wind, especially in times of hunger.
When a thief stole our food, they hung
a dying elder. Compare that to when
Coneconam ended a gambling argument

by executing his own brave, the strongest of men.
They could have learned from my father
who returned an English boy and sent Squanto
to save them, his retaliation for Witawamet's head.

FROM THE BEGINNING, we were free to forage
and splash along the river's portage,
our flesh drying on the ledges of glacial ruins
or soothed in the kettle ponds that hid us

from fierce Tarratines and Narragansetts
below the ocean's arm. Then, the granite hills
above the streams we farmed were still
thick with moose, bear, and beaver, the waters

filled with our women, our tribes made one
lodge against obvious danger. It was Massasoit's dream
that his children would gather wild berries,
and dance like clouds of circled smoke

in peace and loyalty, our only fortress
even with the English not far away.
Montaup had no invasion to fear,
just as Plymouth was free from our spears.

But in my dream last night I saw
the black markings in the birch
and the dark tips of a hawk's wing
winter honed and swooping.

A terror returns like loud carrion
nesting in the meadows above our corn,
calling all wrens and starlings
to plant strange seeds that turn

the bread grain into fences and barns.
Today, many of Kitchtan's people wear
the raven's cloak and his hooked beak
to thresh the earth. They speak

the carrion's caw. The sky
is one hawk, circling. The day
is the hurricane dawn of nestlings
born into a motherless world.

WE WERE THE LAST of my father's seed, the final
kernels of the cob. Long before Wamsutta and me,
generations past, the others were taken by unnatural
disease. Massasoit was almost sixty years when we

left the womb to meet the sun and birdsounds.
He wanted heirs to share his bounty,
and spared nothing for us. We ruled his house
with naked joy. Our days were full of horseplay,

the nights with tales and dancing. Older, we were
given the education of kings. Our elders were tutors.
Our guides, the spirits of the past and the shining
sparks of sky. At my father's side, we learned

the *sachem*'s many tones—the bow-taught firmness
of decision, the salve of supplication,
the tempered talk of just interrogation,
the many gestures of mockery, and

the stampede cry to move all bony hooves
through stubborn blindness, and rise above
our head-lowered grazing in the sod
to gain the eternal vantage of the gods.

From the squaws we learned backbreaking work
and how to nourish others with scraps of root and bark.
Accompoin taught me strategy in games,
Woonasham devotion to the herd and how to hunt.

From the *pawwaw*, I learned magic—to trust
in dreams and reach beyond sight and self,
to find the door from danger and the antidote
to every poison fang and leaf.

He sent me, a stripling, blindfolded
into the wild to seek the place of knowing—
the source of wind, wet, and warmth—
to discover Nature's power of change.

How frail is this walking darkness—
the leaf stem or corn stalk whose husking
time is always near. Even as a boy
I understood my half-place in creation.

Half-finished, half-sexed with nothing mine
to hoard, I was the nerve leg of the deer
moving season by season to survive. Sensing
danger, I commanded my spirit to rise.

The lift that lightened was pure life,
a force equal to the pull of earth. I soared
with crows above the tree crowns, beyond
loneliness to the great merging where

the world and smoke are one—like the tremor
of the drumhead, which is thunder
and crackling flame and feet dancing
the first dance under the bow-faced moon.

But at night, we watched the townsmoke
moving closer to cloud the heavens
like the black coats that darkened our trails.
At first our enemy was Miantonomi, who took

Ossamequin prisoner for the greatest ransom known.
The older Wampanoags feared Narragansett arrows
and reprisals while the younger said it was from
English houses and not *weetos* that the poison came.

The English showed more dignity to their dogs
than to our chief, whose spirit, once a spreading fire,
became a frail ember, and nature followed his disposition.
Soon he was too weak to walk. In his eightieth year,

Massasoit lay dying in his hut, unresponsive
to the dried currants and potions in the *pawwaw's* bag.
To my brother and me, he spoke his vision:
"You who have been friends since birth, and walk

in step like horses on a long journey, it is your time
to lead. Pursue the hard road of peace and compromise.
Protect the corn and children. When justice is your guide,
the gods will be with you and ease the burden.

Your ancestors will come to you in need, deliver you
to safe ground, give you words to speak,
for when our people are in your thoughts,
their will is manifest and will come with aid—

as strategy, tool, or weapon. Their will is the surging tide
that lifts us, that gives common men the strength
of Maushop to move boulders and hills."
Wamsutta put his face to our father's head

and aligned his vision with Massasoit's eyes.
He took the king's mantle, and I the string
of wampum from his neck. We felt like imposters,
as if we were now wearing English clothes.

We were young. How could two colts
lead ten thousand men? But in my dream
I flew with my father's spirit to bear
Wamsutta up the slope of Wachusett.

The rooks came to help us.
This is the truth of dreams,
the wing flight that takes us beyond
two worlds to the familiar unfamiliar.

THEN WE WERE PROUD to take English names.
I rode with my brother and fifty braves into Plymouth,
and was greeted with gawps of wonder, the English
anxious to see the pups who ruled the pack.

In their longhouse, we made a new pact
of friendship, and, to celebrate, smoked tobacco,
while one of their chiefs gave us new titles.
"Wamsutta, henceforth you shall be Alexander,

conqueror of many tribes of Europe and Asia.
Metacom, you shall be Philip, after the king
of Macedon, another great ruler." I felt honored,
not the butt of a joke, the younger brother named

for the father. And so we left their great city
of wooden walls as triumphant as if we, too,
were conquerors. On the way home, we thought
of the good we took away. The shared oaths of loyalty

made us safe from the Naragansetts, Mahicans
and the hatchet-toothed Tarratines, who,
in the season of falling water, invaded our camps
ravenous for food and women. We would be spared

the soldier's bullet. Our worries were the proximity
of towns and farms and the sailors' sickness
that emptied our villages. And as the days
and harvests passed in their own procession,

from the rutting of foxes and the season of cherries
to the mellowing of the vine apple, I took slowly
to my new position, ripening in confidence
as a judge and advisor to my brother.

I did not seek this post.
I was more ready to run the meadow
and to hunt moose and bear than
to mold the will of men at a council fire.

It was the season of ripe fruit when I went
with Wamsutta to drink tea from the white gourd
in that English dwelling. We had sold land
to Providence, but others wanted what still was ours.

Winslow came to Montaup with an army of guns
to take Alexander to Plymouth to explain.
Though my brother was sick with fever, Weetamore
urged her husband to travel, bringing a great entourage.

I was with him when he was forced to sign their treaty,
with him as his angry belly rebelled, tied in knots
of agony as at a birth. The whiskey did not help.
We put him on a toboggan behind my horse,

and I pulled him over miles of road and
mowed fields to ease his pain. His final thoughts
were of our people. "Think first
of the children and the helpless ones.

Keep them from harm
and every tribe will follow
like a litter over smooth grass."
Barely a man, I was then a king.

AGAIN THE SAGAMORES CAME with gifts in tribute—
immeasurable words and grain, wealth
worn on their backs as frail amulets against
the club that beats down fathers and brothers,

bringing tribes together in remembrance. My uncles
Accompoin and Annawan, now my charges,
begged the Great Spirit that every hill
bend to me like a horse at the river—

and that the mountain's spine,
its mane of pine and boulders narrowing
into a tail of willow grass, hide me in retreat.
I stood above them, like Wachusett,

distant and disturbed as on my wedding day,
for now I was the hillside they walked on
so they could climb despite youth or frailty
in old age. I was their Kitchtan,

the final word and protector, their winter
and spring. Their glances made me older
than years, asked me what more I could give
like the berries in the field, offering myself

in sustenance and sweetness as a substitute
for anything they lacked. My wife, twice a princess,
was now a queen. My double sister
carried the burden of her loss with dignity

giving Wootonekanuske new strength.
Others wept, but she showed me
all that matters of riches—how to stand
against the riptide of fortune.

Weetamore was with me. We could not hide
our rage. We knew their poison killed Wamsutta,
though the soldiers called it seizure,
the heat conspiring with his temper.

"What do they expect?" I ask her.
"Our young warriors want to avenge
my brother and the bleeding of their
lands, the theft of their furs, the trampling

of our crops by cattle the colonists refuse
to pen, our suffering in stocks for doing
what we have always done—
riding horses or holding a gun."

My urge is to fight the urge to fight
and take my father's path of peace,
never to wear the paint of *mischquock*.
War is no way to gather harvest.

But what do I say to the soldiers who mistake
our mourning—the month-long display
of grief and tribute from every tribe—
as a plot against them? Our worst success

is dreaming in their minds we are dangerous,
and now I must fight from two sides—
against Shoshanim's tongue, searing me
for not showing teeth against our oppressor,

and the soldiers who expect an attack
though none is planned. Our young warriors
want to fight, our old to protect what we have,
though we own nothing but our skins.

And we are powerless until we heal
the rifts between our tribes.
I must eliminate all cause for quarrel
and reunite the river people with the salt.

At first I ignore the request to meet at Plymouth.
Accompoin, afraid the soldiers mean more poison,
is my guide: "In soft winds and dew
we see the mounting storm.

So these soldiers think you gather force.
Let them know half your mind, the sorry
half that weeps with memories of another time,
when we were all together as brothers, and

sovereigns respected *sachems* and feasted together.
Much good came from gathering food to help
the steel helmets weather those first winters."
So I resist again the urge to unleash arrows,

but pray that one day the English, too, shall be forced
to give up land. This I think, but dare not speak
when I stand in their wooden hall,
summoned by soldiers to address the wan faces

in their great house, to face the somber looks
in black robes. They bully me through a gauntlet
of charges and meet my answers with glares
that say, "You are a liar and take us for fools."

The dead sober grow more diabolical in collective.
They accuse me of talking to my own councilors.
"Did you not meet with the *sagamores* to plot
against us? Did you not call for insurrection?"

"I am their *sachem*," I respond. "Do we fault
you blackcoats for gathering on holy days
or your chiefs for convening in your towns?"
Once more I must swallow my anger

like a fish on a pebbled hook, hung naked
and diminished in mid-air. I sign their papers,
turn over guns. Soon, the world will know
who the fools are within these chambers.

YOUR NAME WILL BE LOST, but your stride
guides mine. At eight, the short-haired hunter
already knows to release the taught string
only after the wolf is sated with the venison.

He holds all time in his glance
and will bless the sacred bones
he kills. But today his sapling arrow
misses its target in the gustwind.

O, may he have time for failure.
I withhold my forces till this nameless one
can know his mind and weigh others
before my name will send bullets after him.

THE GRAIN WATER MAKES us louder.
Boisterous speech and laughter, like smoke,
fills the *weetos*, the day recounted the way
a child relives its wonder as he dreams.

"Am I bewitched by an evil spirit?
I know a thousand words and can give
names to a thousand things, yet I let
a squaw-born Christian sign away

my land, bequeathing to himself all I own,
and trusted him to carry out my will.
And how can what is written, true or false,
matter more than speech? The word is god,

and when scribbled is law, though the air
that hears my voice is purer than paper
and remembers more than any man can know.
And how could he take the *weeto* next to mine,

and sleep there upon my niece's breast—
and trick me months later to guarantee
our future to his care? Of course, I must
admit, today, he has received his dowry.

Thank you, friends, for serving me well
and for teaching who to trust. The English
care only for a book, this bible
that taints strong minds with evil spells.

And what did he, for his learning, know?
To take foreign ways and turn on us?
Who holds deed to the seasons?
Time and place cannot be sold

by any signature. Our mark is how we live.
Now they want every last rifle.
Better to take our limbs or pull every tooth
than be helpless against them and the Mohegans."

For years I vowed to stay away from them,
but every year they built more fences
to keep us from the land our *sachems*
sold for trinkets, shells, and paper.

Yesterday they hanged my three men
in the square for no wrong. The white pelts
had declared them guilty of killing
the turncoat, when I, not the Christian

council and its false witnesses, dispense Indian justice.
And when they hanged my advisor and his son,
the rope gave and the boy ran squealing like a piglet
in a snare. They shot him in violation of their law.

But we, too, are to blame for being unready
for the long hunt. We must feign weakness
till we learn to fight again, live on *nókehick*
and rise from the swamps in surprise.

In that season of long shadows, the moon
went dark for the time it takes a log to burn,
a portent of evil, recalling the English
setting the Pequots on fire—to all a grievous

memory. I lift my people's spirits: "The night
has swapped places with the day as Habbomocko
changes faces from friend to foe. But wait.
The brightness will return. Kitchtan will send

Cheapie on his way and chasten the trickster.
Stay with me and watch the sun return—
a good omen." But the *pawwaw* saw no harmony:
"Hearken to me. It is the ash of the Pequots

burned at Mystic. There's a scalp in the sky,
the charred flesh of the death fire. We must release
the black smoke from our guns, and flex our bows
with onyx stone, turning young wives into widows."

I counter with my dream of last night: "Two warriors
of unequal strength battled, and the gods protected
the weaker, who had refused to shed first blood.
Let us be the last to fire, for we will be judged

by our deeds of patience, not of war." The real test
was to bring in allies, and enact my plan,
and though a band of raiders looted Swansea,
they did not raise a gun. An English boy

first shot my warrior. The child was next day
killed, his family's limbs and entrails
strewn along the roadside with those of cattle
and pigs as a totem for soldiers to cart away.

WHEN DID THIS WAR BEGIN? Can we know
which drop of rain begins a squall?
Only that it comes hard, and scatters men,
spreading its darkness like the eye wind

that turns the ocean upside down,
Habbomock thundering his cloud clash
as rash partisans club each other brainless,
while women and children thresh the grain.

I WANTED SEVERAL SEASONS to gather arms
from Mauntaup to Pennacook, and train
with Nipmuck warriors, still fresh
from two wars, but I could not rein

in the young bucks, their raucous energy
more valuable than plans. Nor could I contain
their lust for revenge to burn
the barns and blacken fields. I could not cool

their blood at Taunton or Middleborough,
but at Rehoboth and Dartmouth I rebuked them,
saying "War is won by discipline, not pleasure,
and by what we lose or gain, in equal measure."

Then my warriors began to heed
my command like saddle horses,
willing to turn or gallop at my lead
to prevent more senseless losses.

THEY CALL ME KING, but I have no subjects
to pay me tribute like the English crown,
which demands the last vestige of my authority—
so powerful is the throne across the sea!

A *sachem* can only beseech
his tributaries in supplicant speech
for their continued trust,
and plead with Nature thus:

Spirit of beaver, quahog, moose,
answer my call. We have traded you,
great givers, and your secret lairs
for strings of wampum *deep as the ocean.*

From you, who feed us, we ask in prayer:
Before the leaf turns and the sands no longer
hold the glare of sun, and the air breathes
cold as wave, make the land ours once more.

When the geese go southward
and the red fish run to sea and the bone
soup is boiled to sinew, make the land
free once more. When the shade's broad

hands cease to cover and we cache
our extra corn for winter food, we ask
your relief. Givers of life and sustenance,
before the leaf falls, make the land free

once more, if only to blanket our sons
with tarps of grass for your safekeeping.
We will paint our faces for lasting sleep
and pay any price to restore this land.

THE CORMORANT SWIRLS in the wind
uncertain whether to land or fly. The sun
has left our sky. Woonasham,
protecting our flank, has fallen.

Soon, the English will come
with that dog Uncas to Pokanoket,
tracking us faster than we can run.
We must flee our tents, brooks, this millet,

taking only the clothes on our backs.
Torch the stacks of your best harvest.
Scatter your *wampum* in the foxtails.
We must leave even our memories.

This is as it should be. If we hold ground,
Henchman will quarter us and our land,
parceling what remains like fingers
of corncake for the white children.

Brother, take the frail ones to Ninigret.
Braves, we will enter Nipmuck
and burn their forts along the river
till the swamps fill with blood.

They build better than they fight
and will return with more men
like Tarratines, taking our scalps
with every treaty we sign.

They will not rest until our children
barter our thirty-nine gods for their bearded one.
They could take us now, but Uncas
will stop for these trinkets.

My son, the time is coming when you will fight,
and your words will carry the weight of spears
and it will be yours to decide who lives or dies
and when to quit the battle. But for now, wait.

You will face their weapon's thunder
and give courage to your men, and sit
with enemies to plan our fate, full of hope,
though unsure if you will last the night.

You will see beyond the farthest wave
and know the course when the chop
is rough, choosing what is best for all.
You will stare at danger with the wisdom

of Akkompoin, and teach others patience,
justice, and respect for the trickster,
resilient to every shift of fortune.
But for now, wait until you ride three hands

higher than the rest, dressed in my robes
and the feathered comb of chief.
This day will mend. The bloody field
will once again bear fruit.

TO MAKE THE SAFE STEP in the dark is wisdom,
not cowardice. The whites were gutless,
hesitating (though they could have finished me)
and whining that I always hid and ran.

Captain Church, leaving Mosely's ship,
stumbled into my war party at Pocasset.
We charged his company, their worn-out guns
either lacked bullets or misfired.

Church ran for the sloop, sailing to Plymouth
for Henchman's army, returning with others
and soldiers on horseback to push us deep
into the swamp. We burrowed like quahogs,

a living mud of bubbling bramble. We became
the woods and stream, invisible to soldiers
who lost heart for hunting. Henchman
believed he could starve us in our element.

Behind me, the sea spoke in a great roar:
The loud waves will cover your escape.
Follow me at low tide, tying yourselves
to the floating lengths of trees.

We moved before sunrise, afraid
the soliders might back us into the waves
like pigs for gelding. Wading over oyster beds,
the flotilla of 100 braves lying on trunks of pines

mastered the surf that reared beneath us
like wild horses. Down current
we floated unnoticed till Rehoboth where
Weetamore offered salve and refreshment.

I SEE MOST CLEARLY after twilight when
the farmers' sheep and cows are hidden
in their pens and the land is restored.
My heart soars higher than smoke.

Above, the moon is small, a conch medallion
the sky goddess wears. We ride in the shadows
of trees, a moving mass of darkness fat as hills.
Tonight, we will gather more horses,

and torch the houses till the smoke is thick
as the afterburn of harvest, sickly sweet
and hotter than Monoco's tongue.
Bravest before battle, he and Muttawmp,

my war captain, excite the men with visions of glory.
The Nashaway recounts his fight with a two-headed
English god. "I rode toward the bad medicine
as he put his white mane inside his breeches.

The other head aimed his pistol at my good eye.
'Do you barter, Indian? My wig for your head.'
and I hissed: 'What magic have you, two-faced one?
Shoot, and I will scalp you to the cheek,'

I rode at him, the one they call Mosely.
His bullet missed my jaw by a finger's width. I flung
my tomahawk at his forehead to leave my mark.
Next time, he'll remember One-eyed John."

Muttawmp of the Quaboags has plotted an ambush
for the British captains who came to negotiate
for our guns. It is all planned—the attack
on Brookfield, and the surprise on the officers

at the one-shoulder pass. Dusk hides
the smoke when we burn Brookfield,
the braves scrambling for remaining stores.
I look behind at the ember village, the fort

a falling fence of flame, and think how Kitchtan
speaks without words, and stands with us
against the invaders. If only our cousins
would join—the Narragansett, the Sakonett,

the Pennacook—deaf to us, stay allies
to braves and soldiers even as they are sent
to Deer Isle for sharing our blood.
We fight for them, too.

Monoco captures three farmers with guns,
burying them to their necks: "Let them face the sun
and rise like plants to replace us," he crows.
At sunup we ride to Hatfield to strike again.

HOW POORLY THEY FIGHT, these Englishmen.
Their numbers are large. If they had wise
chiefs, or sense, they would pin us down.
Instead, they send their troops to patrol

the swamps, or build useless fortresses.
Near the river's bend, Muttawmp displays
his force with fire. Hadley burns,
calling Pynchon to send his soldiers

to meet him. Meanwhile, a tribe once friendly
to the English burns the biggest prize of all.
The Agawams take the garrison at Springfield,
and the town falls into our hands like rain.

We know their movements, but who has learned
our ways? Who can make sense of our raids,
or beat us back? Only men of peace—
Eliot and our neighbor, Providence.

“WE, TOO, ARE PEOPLE of faith,
though we do not erect crosses to the sky
or hang neighbors from on high
as demonstrations of strength.

We do not force our tribes to sacrifice
work for an insecure god, who like the sky
will crack and strike, forcing the flock
into pens or the safety of stockades–

or build, as you have, other colonies
that allow divergence from this love.
We carry our homes on our backs
and are bowed only by this earthly trek.

We speak true. What we say, we mean.
Our words are not knives that cut
the throats of our prey. We have lived here
longer than memory, and could have killed

the first settlers, but gave them food, bartered seeds
and knowledge of the land, out of goodness,
only to be repaid by deadly arrogance,
steaming mounds of words and lies.

Their language is *quequécum*, a foul wind.”
This I speak to Roger Williams, who is fair
and as different from the others as Niantics
from Mohawks. “When we are not one mind,

the world is out of balance,” he says, and
softly disputes my claims about his god,
though he will not defend his countrymen.
“My cousins are hard masters who have lost

their ears. Their voices have gone shrill
and cold. Tell me what I can do."
He comes as a man of the god of all men,
not just the English. He sleeps in my hut,

unafraid. It is no longer up to me, I explain.
"We do what we must to stand straight.
We talk, we sing, we dance.
We fight, we die, and it is done.

We stand firm in what we know:
the earth is a great hearth that brings
forth the flavored shoots to feed the open
wound of summer. The song-filled sky

carries the sacred crow southwest
to the source of sunlight and corn.
We move with the seasons like birds,
becoming one flock in harmonious flight.

This is the destiny that is ours,
but you must not fear. Not a hair
on your head will be harmed.
This is my word. I have spoken."

NO TEST OF FAITH CAN TELL who is
friend or foe. Oaths and treaties
break easily. The trickster chooses
at whim who will wear his mask.

The Agawams turned on Pynchon
just as my secretary became Uncas,
and Uncas turned in Miantonomo
for one cause—to buzzard the carcass

of their brothers for more land. Trust
in Habbomock and you'll see....
Traitors sack our winter corn.
Soldiers fight as the weather hardens.

My horse is tired, and the trackers close
on me like wolves, their fangs bared
as musket blades. Winter blows
piercing cold from the bleak hills.

My braves gorge and maw
the grist of cattle our raids bring.
They whoop like birds, their mighty wings
spread in flapping victory. I know the thaw

will come too late and the feast will end
too soon. The drifts of Albany's winter,
peaking above laurels, show we have lost
our way, our tribes scattered like the bones

we gnaw and throw away, the last remnants
of the blood orgy. Springfield is rebuilt.
I must ask Canonchet to join our cause,
though I'm afraid our plan to reunite

Nipmuck and Narragansett has hatched too late.
We cannot drive the English to the sea,
nor live beside them through another eighty winters.
If only I could be a child again and let my father carry

the fate of our people like a child in his arms.
I am a fading ember beneath his star.
I cannot end the bloody feast. So I paint
my face with ashes and cranberries.

QUINNAPIN KNOWS THE PAIN of plenty.
I chose just one, she whose red cap
caught my eye, and whose beadwork
spoke of finery. *Nowéewo*, I thought instantly.

Kitchtan tossed away the stones
and from a fragrant, nutty tree
carved my form, my heart,
and this Wootonekanuske.

I studied the cloth belt that was her modesty.
My eyes traced the rise of her bosom beneath
the wisps of black hair, soft as cornsilk.
She embodied ripeness, the swell of harvest,

and a strength to carry a *sachem*'s worries
in her small basket. *Wootonekanuske*,
I said her name and smiled, knowing
that in her presence work would be done.

Her hands were hardened from digging shells,
and pushing a needle through hides.
Her voice was a soft stitch
that drew me to her side;

her hair a flying arrow,
a feather of bird-light indigo;
her flesh a winter's meal—
all I would need to survive.

O give me rest and sanctum,
and spell me in your clutching arms.
My heart was bent and shaken;
I was so taken with her charms.

TODAY I SPOKE with the prayer man's wife,
Mary Rolling Sun, whose hair and spirit
are as fiery as Weetamore's vanity.
It takes my sister a whole morning to dress.

How does Quinnapin stand it?
I give the red hair bear gruel and three
shillings to sew leggings for my son.
Perhaps she will remember this,

and speak of me well, for soon I will
ransom her for the cost of rifles.
I will speak well of her, for the deacon
might easily believe Monoco's lies.

To taunt the soldiers, he claims
she has become his wife and will not return
to her husband—or any house
other than the hut of One-Eyed John.

I SEE MY FEARS in the barren trees,
our stores spent, my stallion tired
and gaunt, each step trampling
the first shoots of spring.

As we ride, my men mask
our tracks on the trails upland.
I have one hope and task:
to beg the Narragansett to stand

with me in this death treaty.
I will seal my bond with Canonchet,
who for two thousand fathoms might slit
my throat but would kill a British

major for half, for we are friends.
Last summer, we swore allegiance.
As the sky has a pact with river and rain,
we will join forces to drive the pox

toward sunrise and the mighty sea.
The great Ocean will stand with the sky.
Two enemies will become one army,
bound together to be free.

Tahínash waupanash ...
How many winds are there
that can blow against us?
North, North East, East,

Southeast, West, Northwest ...
But no pleasing warmth from the place
where the corn was born and the souls
of our departed dwell with the *manitou.*

The hardened heart of winter gusts
from the mouth of every messenger,
from warm friends met on the road side
offering tobacco. We greet each other.

"What news have you?" and Habbomock,
the messenger, tells me: "Your great wish
has been granted. What you will, you do.
To make war, Canonchet will stand with you.

But he has lost fortress and family. Indian Peter
led soldiers into his island fortress, through
the tight-thighed entrance of the labyrinth
that was his nation's shield. Hundreds fell

entering or defending the womb. Soldiers
on their bellies crawling with flintfire
forced the last defenders to the blazing huts.
Yotáanit opened his arms to embrace the squaws,

who shielded, then smothered, their babies
to keep them from flames and lead. Flesh ash,
death stink, the walls to keep the English at bay
holding heat like a kiln. Bullets spraying,

slaying every motion to the last child.
No edifice, no Stone John fortress
of words can describe the carnage.
No ocean of weeping can mourn it."

The messenger says that the coat men squabble
over the spoils. "Boston would invade Providence
if not for the freethinkers who are harder devils
to manage than Narragansetts. I have heard a tale

that they hanged three women made liquor crazy
by their god and that a man from Pawtucket
was arrested for molesting his milk cow.
Boston was so horrified, it renounced its claim

to Providence. But what did they expect?
If you kill the tribe's young women, the men
will seek some outlet." The messenger speaks true.
He is done with his news and my tobacco.

NEVER HAVE I SEEN HIM look so tall and fierce,
my rival, son of the great chief Miantonomi,
standing like Maushop, who hurled
the boulders that formed our mountains and lakes

and keeps all predators away. "Metacom,
we meet each other at last, equal and unvanquished,
the great tribes of the land, the headwaters of the last
streams. Now we join forces with the *Manitou*.

Let Habbomocko, who has tricked me
into despair, show me the way to vengeful joy.
Teach me how to raid their sleeping fortresses,
and mislead their guides across familiar pathways.

Let us wreak havoc on every village,
and hurl thunderbolts to clear more fields.
There is no time to weep,
and much weeping to deliver."

But hard as he tries, Canonchet cannot ravage
enough villages to relieve his hurt.
We fight without discipline. This is not war,
only our own reckless, isolate terror visited

on highways and homesteads, a spreading fire.
Indians forget their bonds to their *sachems*
and attack anyone for food or ransom.
People without gods, history, faith, and future

run like me, with no place to go, no home
to return to. We lack a center, lack hope,
and our last calls for help have turned
against us. Now the man-eating Mohawks—

helping Governor Andros lay claim to our lands—
have attacked us from our own stronghold.
The losses are great. Friends and protectors
bleed into the red roots of the sumac.

WE GLIDE THE PLEASANT waters
as a child plays snake in snow.
Each stroke is an arrival,
changing the forest as we go.

The sun remakes the surface
and glints beneath our oars.
We skim the water's foaming,
sweat rolling as we steer.

We move like a sewing needle,
dipping in lengths along the shore,
to beach near the shining waters,
where three hundred plunged the falls

or were shot in their slumber by Holyoke
and Turner. They, too, lie here forever—
slain by the sleepers' brothers,
the roughest knives of war.

From loss, all is made—
my hut, the scalp of trees;
my life's tobacco glow, a dying ash
fanned with my fading breaths.

My smoke is small, a force
that warms and irritates at once.
I sing with burning throat from
a pipe which knows no peace.

My restless sleep is broken
by thought's charges and retreats.
My heart is the hard buckhorn
of a deer slaughtered for its meat.

Our hunger, like a hunter, propels us
through the Great Swamp's unwakened
dead. I weep tears of dew and sunlight
for the black night to end.

But the English fences walk the corn
and stalk the wind. The big spars
and rising spires are turning spits
that pierce the sacred from the world.

No magic puff will cure
or protect this bone and reed.
I breathe the singeing breath
that will not cease with death.

Spirits, i hear you sing in water sizzling
on this stone, jumping like a war dance
beneath the painted sky, the sweat lodge thick
with steam and pipesmoke and sweet fern

rubbings to cover my scent from predators.
I fan the pit of fire, seated by the stone altar
where magic herbs and water steam the hearth.
The air is fresh and fragrant as after rainfall.

The steaming stone responds to the smoke-making fire,
turning one form of life to another.
My heart has stopped. My wife and son are captives.
The last stalwarts—save for Annawon—are dead.

Lay down these names finally and forever: Canonchet,
captured gathering cornseed from the burnt swamp;
Weetamore, my second love, drowned in her bay;
Accompoin shot at my feet while my last sentinels

traded me for a crust. What next?
Kitchtan saved me from the *netop* rifle that missed me
by a moment's indecision. But Church's army of Pocassets
knows where every oyster sleeps. No bed is safe.

I do not want to shame the gods, but today,
I shot a deserter. His brother will bring
soldiers here. I have only time to curse,
the strength for this last strike:

May the enemy find its own defeat in mine
and one day have to sell—or poison—their lands
to slake their unquenchable thirst for more.
My body sweats like a rutting animal.

My spirit flies like a leaf on the wind,
let loose from branch and trunk, feeling
the helve mark where the axe
cut down my loved ones at the ankles.

Soon I, too, will shed the taste
of my own dead skin. The dogs
swirl the woods. The buzzards circle.
Soon my own scent will betray me.

THE ENGLISH HOLY MEN CALL for the death of my wife
and son, as good Gookin, Providence, and Church
beg to secure such mercy as they can extend
(the prizes of war sent in irons to the Indies).

The daughter and bride of kings will be led
through a pompous trial and packed
for Tortolla to fill a white planter's bed.
My son will work the rum fields.

I can only pray that he will return like Samoset
and help the lost ones find their way.
If I have hurt anyone, it is my family
and tribal harmony.

Why did we live to know this?
Would it have been better never to see
this day, better to miss the shade of oaks
and the oyster beds at Mayhew's walk?

Being alive, we have everything to lose.
Children, nation, pride—all vanish like the tide
coming fast with open arms only to flee from us
like a false friend. So, too, do the seasons pass.

We travel the many rounds of weather
unsure of how far we'll go, or what will be our
finest moments, or what decree or blight
will bring us down, or what bright luck

may lengthen the twilight's shadow
that clears the heavens to sparkle with our gods.
Each day is a quiet note we beat upon the earth,
but our lives are a sudden storm, bursting

from the clouds with a thunderous roar,
ravaging the ridge of earth, riding the wind
in many directions, here and there,
along the different paths we make.

This is our dusk, People of the Dawn.
Many days were ours, but tomorrow
is Kitchtan's. It will come without us,
as the night flares of the heavens become

the shining light, as the sea's dredgings
help the corn to rise, and the dead seed
will yield new crops. From here, the crow
will carry us like the first bean and kernel

to the origins of the sun, where time fades
and lifetimes blend like change of day,
and the spirits dance their pictures
in others' dreams. My voice grows faint

from sadness for the lost tribes, the carrier
birds which vanished like clouds, and
the hoofdust of the herds we chased
to the final fencebreak. I have shouted

my last buckscree. I wear Katahdin's colors
no more. You can hear me among the spirits
if you listen well, though I know not what
to say or what the dead foretell.

CROW, BRING THIS MESSAGE to my son.
Carry the eagle feather to him as he sails.
This frail and tiny leaf once signified
a man the gods once unduly favored.

YOU KNEW IT WOULD BE here and now,
swamped and cornered like a pig at the spear,
when you would finally hear me, Kitchtan,
sachem of the gods, who created this moment

and stands with me before gun and lance,
unmovable, even by my gratitude.
O most helpless and unhelpful One,
I stand with you. It is your death I mourn,

for with this last smoke of breath
your people are no more, each tribe
treatied to its slaughter, our women taken
in irons on Mosely's ship to the islands.

It was all foreseen by you. You understood
what happens when tow paths are cut
through the same wood. It's Cheapie's law—
the extreme takes over, the pathways merge

and widen until the last tree falls.
Walk with me, released of your burden.
I am your prisoner. Do not tie me.
Kitchtan, your courage makes this last gesture

seem small. I will face my murderer Indian,
and his brothers' hatchets will spill my blood
until I cannot speak. No matter.
My actions are words, and even so cannot express

my love for my people, and for you who gave us
sunlight and corn, who falls with each death
like the cut stalk and the day's shadow.
Thank you, good soldier, for finding me.

ENDLESS IS THE FUSE of war
that binds our way to clash
and maim like jousting bucks
til we meet our pointed end.

The death fields flood with silty hate.
Where is the coward who in courage
calls "Enough"? How can we douse
this self-fueling flame?

What excuse cannot be made
to save a world ablaze?
The fuse of war is life, slithering
toward its end like a hissing snake.

My life, a lonely squall, has passed. My words,
thunder stripped of heat and light, are
carried now in the street chatter of crows
who move the dead remains with their raucous

chorus, my only eulogy. Crow, holiest of birds,
carry these words, the seeds of my being, to open air.
Bring my heart into the *weetos* and fill each bed
with my tale, for once again Habbomock rules,

and the blessed songs of work are the drums of war,
and justice falls like dust on now forgotten trails,
and the believers spread a gospel hate
while the sensible will not wear Katahdin's paint.

The rook has fallen from its roost.
Who will speak for him and carry
Kitchtan's blessings, or clean
the fetid bones with his beak?

Who will shout my indignation across this now
conscripted land? The wings of air swirl and go.
What is that howling in the hills? The grey fences
are wolves, posted like sentries, watching us.

Endnotes

Pages 13, 14

Massasoit (1580-1660), also known as Osamequin, father of Philip (Metacom) and Alexander (Wamsutta), who presided over a long period of peace with the colonists.

Sachem, also known as **Sagamore**, the tribal chieftain, who typically inherited power by lineage and maintained it through the consent of the people and other tribes who paid tribute for protection. This post required outstanding leadership and diplomatic skills. The sachem served as a mediator in disputes and chief negotiator with other tribes, and presided over the council of wise men, elders, and clan heads. The *sachem* was usually the wealthiest man or woman in the tribe.

Wampanoags, an Alonquian tribe whose name means "People of the East" or "People of the Dawn," once were a close ally of Plymouth colony. Based between Fall River, Mass., and Providence, R.I., the tribe ruled over the New England confederation of Algonquian tribes that once included nearly 20,000 people. The Wampanoags and their allies were virtually wiped out in King Philip's War.

Metacom (1638–1675), alias Metacomet or King Philip, sachem of the Wampanoags, second son of Massasoit and brother of Alexander, or Wamsutta.

Montaup, called by the English "Mount Hope," the ancestral homeland of the Wampanoag sachems, which was located on a small peninsula in Rhode Island Sound in what is now Warwick, R.I.

Mathers refers to Increase Mather (1630-1723), Puritan clergyman and president of Harvard College, author of *A History of the War with the Indians* (1676), and Cotton Mather (1663-1728), his son, who became one of the most celebrated New England Puritan ministers and later helped stir up the wave of hysteria that led to the Salem witch trials.

Colonel Samuel Mosely, a former Barbary pirate who was commissioned as an officer in the colonial army and was notorious for his unwarranted violence toward the Indians.

Pokanoket, which means "The Place of the Clear Land," was the principal headquarters of the Wampanoag sachems, located in what is now Bristol, R.I.

Sakonnet, Indian tribe near Mount Hope, whose squaw sachem, Awashonks, helped the colonial forces capture Philip.

Captain Benjamin Church (ca. 1640-1718) colonial soldier, who criticized British tactics in King Philip's War and ultimately decided to employ Indian braves as scouts, which was the major tactical turning point. Church captured Philip's family in August 1676 and, with the help of the Sakonnets, tracked down and killed Philip at Mount Hope.

Nummeneshánnantam!, an Algonquian word meaning "I scorn" or "I take indignation."

Manitou, the Algonquian word for the spirits that inhabited the world and the gods who ruled over the heavens and earth.

Page 15

Coneconam, *sachem* of Manomet (Sandwich), who had friendly relations with the colonists and helped return to his home a Plymouth boy who had been lost in the woods. He advised other tribes on how to deal with the English, with whom he signed a treaty in 1621. Miles Standish distrusted him for being too close to Wituwamet, a Massachusetts sachem who had sworn to overthrow the Plymouth colony. (See Wituwamet.)

Squanto, a Patuxent brave who was captured by English soldiers, sent to England, and sold as a slave in Spain. He escaped to England and returned to America in 1619. Sent by Samoset to Plymouth as an interpreter and guide, he was the colonists' savior. When his tribe was completely wiped out by smallpox he joined the Wampanoags, where Massasoit employed him to befriend the Plymouth colony. Squanto later became a source of tension between the colonists and the Wampanoags, because he used his power to threaten other tribes and to undermine Massasoit.

Wituwamet, sachem of the Massachusetts, who believed the Europeans purposefully brought the plague to New England. He conspired with other tribes to destroy Plymouth but Massasoit revealed the plot to the colonists. Standish and his soldiers killed the sachem, his young brother, and other warriors, and carried Wituwamet's head to Plymouth on a pike. After the incident, the Massachusetts sachem

Chicataubut retaliated by killing three Englishmen who had come to live with him. When Standish ordered that more Indians be killed in retribution, Massasoit stopped the carnage through a gesture of goodwill. He returned a captive English boy who had been staying with the Niantics and sent Squanto to help the starving colonists.

Page 16

Tarratines, also known as the Abnakis, were based north of the Pennobscot River in Maine and Canada and were a scourge of the New England tribes.

Narragansetts, or "The People of the Point," the largest and most powerful tribe in New England, which controlled the land of Narragansett Bay on the east to the Pawcutuck River. The tribe had fought against most other New England tribes in the half-century prior to King Philip's War. Led by Canonicus and Miantonomo and later by Canonchet, the Narragansetts were the long-time enemy of the Pequots and remained neutral in Philip's War until the colonists declared them partisans for harboring Wampanoags.

corn, which in the 17th century referred to any grain–such as wheat, barley, oats, and maize–that was harvested. It is used in this piece to refer, at times, to grain and to maize.

Kitchtan, or Kytan, Kietan, Cautantowwit, or Squantam, the Great Spirit, sachem of the gods, who made heaven, earth, the sea, all the gods, man and woman, and all other creatures.

Pages 18–20

Wamsutta, or Alexander, eldest son of Massasoit, brother of Philip and a husband of Weetamore, became sachem of the Wampanoags in 1660 after his father's death. He died on June 8, 1662 after being summoned from Mount Hope to Plymouth by Major Josiah Winslow. Philip believed Wamsutta was poisoned by Winslow, while many accounts claim that he died of natural causes exacerbated by the journey and Winslow's harsh treatment.

Accompoin, or Unkompoin, Philip's uncle and counselor.

Woonasham, aka Woonashum or Nimrod, was Philip's close friend and counselor. He was killed near Pokaneket at the beginning of the war.

pawwaw, also called powwow, a spiritual leader, shaman, or medicine man.

black coats, also "coat men" or "the coat people"—names given to the English, because they were clothed and wore black coats.

Miantonomi, aka Miantonomo, sachem of the Narragansett, once captured Massasoit and returned him for a king's ransom.

weeto, the conical wigwam prevalent among the Algonquian tribes in New England.

Maushop, a giant who, according to Algonquian legend, gave the New England landscape its topographical features, protected its inhabitants from predatory birds, and generally assisted the Algonquians before the arrival of Europeans.

Wachusett, Mount Wachusett, a meeting place for the Massachusetts Indians, near present day Worcester.

Page 22

Mahicans, a tribe that occupied territory along the upper Hudson River in northeastern New York state and western Vermont. Splinter groups from this tribe migrated across New England and into Connecticut in the late 16th century. These included the fierce Pequots and a rebel faction from that tribe, the Mohegans.

Page 23

Weetamore, also Weetamoo, Weetamo, and Weetimore, the squaw sachem of the Pocassets. She married Wamsutta, Philip's brother, bringing two powerful Wampanoag tribes together. She was also the sister of Philip's wife and later married Quinnapin, a Narragansett chief.

Page 24

Wootonekanosuke, Philip's wife, was the daughter of a Pocasset sachem and the sister of Weetamore.

Page 25

míschquock, a paint the color of red earth used for clothing in peace time and as a war paint in times of conflict.

dreaming in their minds. Refers to the fear the Indians engendered as if they could enter the settler's dreams and frighten them.

Shoshanim, a Nipmuck chief, aka Sagamore Sam, who often challenged Philip's strategy in fighting the English.

Page 28

Your name will be lost. The name of Philip's son is not recorded.

Page 29

Squaw-born Christian, John Sassamon, a Christian Indian educated at Harvard, was tutored by John Eliot and later served as a scribe and counselor to Philip, who came to consider him a traitor for pursuing his own self-interest through double dealing. When Sassamon's body was found in Assawampsett Pond, an Indian who claimed to be an eye-witness to the murder assigned blame to some of Philip's friends, who were executed after an unfair trial. The incident triggered the first hostilities of the war and is the subject of an excellent book, *Igniting King Philip's War: The John Sassamon Murder Trial*, by Yasuhide Kawashima.

Page 30

Mohegans, a tribe based in Connecticut that originally splintered off from the Pequots (see below) and were enemies of Philip and many of the tribes in the New England confederacy.

Page 31

white pelts, English judges and attorneys who wore white wigs in court.

in violation of their law. Under colonial law, if the rope broke during a hanging, a prisoner was to be released. This did not happen in this case.

nókehick, parched meal eaten hot or cold with water that was the regular food of travelers and warriors.

Page 32

The moon went dark. On June 26, 1675 there was a lunar eclipse that was an ominous sign to the Algonquians.

Habbomocko, Abbamococho, Habbomock, Habbomoqui, or Cheepie, the god of deception and chaos, a kind of devil. While less powerful than the supreme deity, he played a significant role in the daily lives of the Algonquians. In the words of John Josselyn, "They acknowledge a god ... but worship him they do not, because (they say) he will do them no harm. But Abbamocho (or Cheepie) many times smites them with incurable diseases, scares them with his apparitions and panic terrors; by reason whereof they live in a wretched consternation, worshiping the devil for fear." (cited *in Indian New England, 1524-1674: A Compendium of Eyewitness Accounts of Native American Life*).

Pequots, Indian tribe headquartered in southern Connecticut and was virtually wiped out when Connecticut soldiers slaughtered hundreds of braves, women and children in 1637.

Swansea, a town in southeastern Massachusetts (est. 1667) that was the site of the first skirmish of King Philip's War, July 24, 1675. A week after two Wampanoags were hung for the murder of John Sassamon, the tribe raided farms at the outskirts of the village. The town itself was founded when the General Court reneged on its agreement to prohibit settlement on native lands.

Page 34

Nipmuck, the "freshwater" Indian tribes located between Mount Wachusett (Worcester) and the Connecticut River. They were close allies of Philip during the war and led many of the raids on the colonial farms and forts in western Massachusetts.

Taunton, a town attacked by Indians in 1675 at the beginning of the war.

Middleborough, a town east of Plymouth and close to Assowompsett Pond where John Sassamon was killed, it was the site of a

Wampanoag raid in late June 1675.

Rehoboth, village in Massachusetts at the headwaters of Narragansett Bay directly across from Providence, it was the site of one of the first attacks in the war and other raids and skirmishes.

Dartmouth, one of the first towns attacked by the Wampanoags to start the war; a place where settlers were murdered, then disemboweled.

Page 36

Uncas, sachem of the Mohegans, who fought on behalf of the colonists in the Pequot War. As part of his plan to become the most powerful chief in New England, he also supported the English against King Philip.

Henchman, Captain Daniel, soldier who early in the war tracked Philip with the aid of the Mohegans. He had numerous opportunities to catch and subdue Philip but was frequently outmaneuvered by him.

Ninigret, sachem of the Niantics, a tribe allied with Philip and based near the Thames River in Connecticut.

Page 38

cowardice, Rev. William Hubbard of Ipswich and other colonists called Philip a coward because he was rarely present in battle. According to Hubbard: "The Fears of the English made Philip nearly Omnipresent, while in reality there is no Evidence that he was present in any Fights along the Connecticut River. He was timid and cowardly, and was continually skulking form Place to Place, and perhaps urged others to fight." (See *Sources.*)

Ran for the sloop. Church wrote a larger-than-life tale of his experience in the war, which includes the following: "But when at last it came to Mr. Church's turn to go aboard, he had left his hat and cutlass at the well where he first came down. He told his company he would never go off and leave his hat and cutlass for the Indians; they should never have that to reflect upon him. Though he was much dissuaded from it, yet he would go fetch them. He put all the powder he had left into his gun (and a poor charge it was) and went presenting his gun at the enemy until he took up what he went for. At his return he discharged the gun at his enemy to bid them farewell, for that time; but had not powder enough to carry the bullet halfway to meet them. Two bullets from the enemy struck the canoe as he went on board; one grazed the hair of his head a little before; another struck in a small stake that stood right against the middle of his breast." (See *Sources*.)

Pages 39, 40

Monoco, aka "One Eyed John," Nashua *sachem*, who, like Colonel Mosely, was much noted for his cruelty in battle and for boasting about it.

Muttawmp, Quaboag brave who led numerous raids in the Nipmuck territory of Western Massachusetts.

two-headed English god. During battle, Colonel Mosely put his wig in his pocket and appeared to the Indians to be a god who could change appearance.

Brookfield, central Massachusetts town, which was attacked in August 1675 and was abandoned for 10 years thereafter.

Deer Isle, located off the coast of Charlestown where Praying Indians were incarcerated and endured—or died of—cold, hunger, and disease.

Let them face the sun. The scene is cited Jill Lapore's *The Name of War*, pp. 95-96. *(See Sources.)*

Hatfield, a village along the Connecticut River between Northampton and Deerfield, which defended an attack by more than 800 Indians on October 9, 1675, and was partially burned on May 30, 1676, and attacked again in June.

Page 41

Hadley, a village in Western Massachusetts founded in 1659, which was Major Treat's headquarters and the site of an Indian ambush in April 1676 and Muttawmp's feigned attack in June of that year.

Pynchon, Colonel John Pynchon, a trader, soldier, businessman, and public servant, he was the son of William Pynchon, the founder of Springfield, the preeminent English town on the Connecticut River.

Agawams, from the Algonquian word meaning "lowland." The

Agawams were a tribe in western Massachusetts based along the banks of the Connecticut River. Although friendly with Colonel John Pynchon and the settlers at Springfield, they attacked and burned the garrison in October 1675.

Eliot, (1604-1790), English missionary in Massachusetts, who translated the Bible into Algonquian and established 14 praying villages in the colony. His Bible and Indian Primer are prime sources of knowledge about Indians in Massachusetts.

Providence, a village in northeastern Rhode Island founded by Roger Williams in 1636, and a term used here for Williams himself.

Page 42

quequécum, Algonquian onomatopoeia meaning "duck," in this case "the quack of a duck."

Roger Williams (ca. 1603-1683), educated at Cambridge to be a minister, Williams immigrated to the Massachusetts colony in 1631. He served as an educator and clergyman, but his unpopular beliefs put him at odds with the authorities. A steadfast supporter of religious freedom and Indian rights, he denied the validity of the Massachusetts charter, challenged the Puritans to acknowledge that they had separated from the Church of England, and declared that civil magistrates had no power over matters of conscience. As a result, he was banished by the General Court in 1635. In the spring of 1636 he founded Providence on land purchased from Canonicus. One of the most remarkable men of his day, Williams was a friend and tutor of John Milton, a translator of the Indian language and interpreter of native culture, a trading post operator, a three time president of Rhode Island, and a religious philosopher, who worked, unsuccessfully, to prevent King Philip's War. For a detailed account of his life, thought, and times. (See *Sources* for Edwin S. Gaustad's *Liberty of Conscience: Roger Williams in America.*)

Page 44

Canonchet (d. 1676), son of Miantonomo and sachem of the Narragansetts, who attempted to stay neutral in the war but ultimately joined Philip's army as his chief war captain.

Page 46

Quinnapin, a Narragansett sachem who was an ally of Philip and a husband of Weetamore. While the Indians were mostly monogamous, like some men of influence, he had several wives.

Nowéewo, an Algonquian word for "my wife."

Page 47

Mary Rolling Sun, Mary Rowlandson (1637-1711), wife of Rev. Joseph Rowlandson, who was taken captive in February 1676 when 400 Nipmucs, Narragansetts, and Wampanoags attacked Lancaster. She became Weetamore's servant and describes friendly meetings with Philip: "During my abode in this place, Philip spake to me to make a shirt for his boy, which I did, for which he gave me a shilling: I offered the money to my master, but he bade me keep it: and with it I bought a piece of Horse flesh. Afterwards he asked me to make a Cap for his boy, for which he invited me to Dinner. I went, and he gave me a Pancake, about as big as two fingers; it was made of parched wheat, beaten, and fryed in Bear grease, but I thought I never tasted pleasanter meat in my life...." (*The Sovereignty and Goodness of God, 1682*, St. Martin's, 1997, p. 83). She was ransomed by Philip in 1676.

Quinnapin knows the pain ..., After Wamsutta's death, Weetamore married a chief who sided with Plymouth during the war, causing her to flee to Narragansett territory where she married Quinnapin. She is described by Rowlandson as a "severe and proud Dame ... bestowing every day in dressing herself neat as much time as any of the gentry of the land: powdering her hair, and painting her face; going with Neck-laces, with Jewels in her ears, and Bracelets upon her hands: When she had dressed herself, her work was to make Girdles of Wampom and Beads."

Pages 49, 50

Tahínash wáupanash ..., from the Algonquian, meaning "How many winds blow?"

Indian Peter, a Narragansett scout caught by General Winslow's army, who, on threat of hanging, revealed the location of the

Narragansett's fort on the swamp island. The scene describes the Great Swamp Fight, a battle on December 19, 1675, that took place when 1,000 men from Connecticut, Massachusetts, and Plymouth under command of Josiah Winslow of Plymouth attacked the fort. The soldiers penetrated the Narragansett palisades on a five-acre island in a giant swamp near present-day West Kingston, R.I., torched the fort, and massacred nearly 100 braves and between 300 and 1,000 women and children.

Yotáanit, the fire god.

Stone John, the stonemason trained by the English who built the nearly impregnable Great Swamp fortress of the Wampanoags.

Milk cow. In 1656, Richard Chasmore was accused of the capital crime of buggery with one of his heifers. (Cited in Gaustad's biography of Roger Williams.)

Pages 51, 52

Mohawks, the Indian nation living west of the Connecticut River in New York and Connecticut, called "man eaters" and "cowards" by the Algonquians. Philip sought to enlist the Mohawks as his allies in the war, but he was outmaneuvered by New York Governor Edward Andros, who, concerned about the fate of his own colony if Philip succeeded, gave the Mohawks arms to attack Philip's troops as they returned from their winter camp in February 1676. The surprise attack accounted for one of Philip's most devastating losses and, perhaps more than anything else, turned the outcome of the war in the colony's favor.

Gov. Edward Andros (1637-1714), Governor of New York from 1674 to 1681, he was a reluctant supporter of the colonial cause, but played a key role in keeping the Mohawks from joining Philip.

Page 53

snake, an Indian game in which children slide a stick with a knobby end through a trough cut in the snow. The child who skids the stick the furthest wins the game.

Page 55

My wife and son are captives. While the authorities demanded the death of Wootonekanuske and her son, Captain Church, Daniel Gookin and Roger Williams asked for mercy. Philip's family was taken on a slave ship to Tortolla to work in the sugar fields.

Lay down these names finally and forever. Accompoin died on July 30, 1676, after being chased by Church's army from Bridgewater in the swamps of Norton and Rehoboth. Meanwhile, Canonchet was captured by Captains Avery and Denison, who offered to spare his life and those of 43 other braves in exchange for full Narragansett surrender. Canonchet refused. His braves were executed on the spot and he was brought to Stonington for trial. Sentenced to death, Canonchet said: "I like it well; I shall die before my heart is soft, or I have said anything unworthy of myself." He asked to be executed by the son of Uncas, the man who had killed his father. According to Nathaniel Saltonstall: "... that all might share in the Glory of destroying so great a Prince ... the Pequots shot him, the Mohegans cut off his Head and quartered his Body, and Minnicrots Men made the Fire and burned his Quarters, and as a Token of their Love and Fidelity to the English, presented his head on a pike." He was executed on April 11, 1676.

netop, Algonquian for friend, i.e., Indian.

Page 60

Until I cannot speak. Philip was killed on the evening of August 11, 1676, at Mount Hope by a Pocasset warrior named Alderman fighting under Captain Benjamin Church's command. According to Rev. William Hubbard: "Philip, like a Salvage [sic] and wild Beast, having been hunted by the English Forces through the Woods, above an hundred Miles backward and forward, at last was driven to his own Den, upon Mount-hope, where retiring himself with a few of his best Friends into a Swamp, which proved but a Prison to keep him fast, till the Messengers of Death came by Divine Permission to execute Vengeance upon him, which was thus accomplished." (Hubbard, A *History of the Indian Wars in New England, 1676*. See 2002 reprinted edition from Clearfield Press, p. 265.) Upon his death, Philip was quartered and beheaded. His right hand was given to Alderman. The head was brought to Plymouth on a pike, where it was displayed for 20 years. Cotton Mather wrote a gruesome eulogy for this moment: "Thus did God break the head of that Leviathan, and give it to be Meat to the People inhabiting the Wilderness, and brought it to the Town of Plymouth, the very Day of their solemn festival."

Sources

We know little about Philip other than the basic facts of his life and the course of his travels. There are few recollections of how he spoke and, of course, scant writings that would allow us to decipher his motivations and moods. Many contemporary accounts were biased, written by clerics and soldiers who considered Philip a demon, if not the devil incarnate.

I have presented the war as a personal one, following its conduct as it might have appeared to Philip. That is because the events of the war itself, fought according to the rules of Habbomocko (the god of chaos and deception), are hard to trace. More importantly, this approach is what poetry is most about—re-creating the human spirit not merely through courage and cunning in battle but through familiar acts of daily life that reveal individuals—and societies—in their wholeness. (We learn as much about Achilles watching him sulk in his tent as seeing him triumph in combat.)

In a few cases, I have knowingly altered facts. For example, Philip's description of his own death borrows details of Canonchet's capture and execution at Stonington. This was done not to confuse the record, but out of a Native American tradition akin to what we call "poetic license," the storyteller embellishing his story in tribute to a friend.

I relied heavily on many sources, including: first person historical accounts; recent authoritative histories of the war; biographies of key colonial leaders; history books for young people; studies of Indian and Algonquian culture, habits, and beliefs; and other materials.

Of particular note is a series of pamphlets, *Legends of the New England Indians, Volumes II, III, IV*, which I purchased on board the U.S.S. Constitution more than 30 years ago. As a series of tales and legends, their historical accuracy may be questioned, but these writings kindled my interest in Philip, and helped me envision key moments in the narrative, most notably King Philip's flight from Montaup and the circumstances surrounding his death—the inspirations for this work.

I relied heavily on Rev. William Hubbard's book, *A History of the Indian Wars in New England* (1676), for an understanding of the colonial attitudes toward Philip and for its accuracy and colorful commentary. Another, more whimsical, though not overly reliable, contemporary account worth investigating is *Benjamin Church's Diary of King Philip's War, 1675-1676.*

I am deeply indebted to two impressive recent histories of the war —Jill Lepore's *The Name of War: King Philip's War and the Origins of American Identity,* which won the Bancroft Prize, and James D. Drake's *King Philip's War: Civil War in New England, 1675-1676*, the source of the map on page 7. These books provide fresh insight into all aspects of the conflict and have helped revive interest in King Philip. They are far more balanced than Douglas Edward Leach's *Flintlock and Tomahawk*, a highly readable narrative account from the colonial perspective. I relied on Yasuhide Kawashima's *Igniting King Philip's War: The John Sassamon Murder Trial* for information about the complex causes that led to war.

Few accounts capture the spirit and the time as well as first-hand reminiscences of encounters with Indians by either captives or English adventurers. Most compelling are Mary Rowlandson's, *The Sovereignty and Goodness of God and Indian New England,* 1524-1674, *A Compendium of Eyewitness Accounts of Native American Life* and William Wood's *New England's Prospect.* I also recommend Washington Irving's character study of Philip in *The Legend of Sleepy Hollow and Other Stories*, which is a highly sympathetic (and somewhat romanticized) treatment that seeks to balance the Puritan views of Philip presented by the Mathers, Rev. Hubbard, and others.

One of the most fascinating accounts of Philip's times in England and America is Edwin S. Gaustad's *Liberty of Conscience: Roger Williams in America.* I also relied on Roger Williams' *A Key to the Language of America* as the source of Native American words (Narragansett) and insight into Algonquian culture.

Two illustrated books by C. Keith Wilbur, MD, provided a sense of the tools and artifacts, and religious practices of the Algonquians: *The New England Indians: An Illustrated Sourcebook of Authentic Details of Everyday Indian Life* and *The Woodland Indians: An Illustrated Account of the Lifestyles of America's First Inhabitants.*

I would be remiss if I did not mention a few books for young people—Robert Cwiklik's *King Philip and the War with the Colonists* and Joseph Roman's *King Philip: Wampanoag Rebel*—that follow Philip closely and put the reader into the spirit of the times. I relied on Roman's book, Alden T. Vaughan's *New England Frontier: Puritans and Indians,* 1625-1675, and other sources cited here as the basis for the notes that follow the poem.

Born in Springfield, Massachusetts, Sheppard Ranbom spent much of his childhood and youth in a landscape replete with reminders of the Algonquian peoples who once populated all of New England. Educated at Colgate University, he has been a journalist, freelance writer, and a public affairs executive. He is the co-founder and president of Communication***Works*** LLC, a national public affairs firm focused on education, youth, and social policy issues. *King Philip's War* is his first book of poetry.